Young Writers 2006 Poetry Competi

"I have a dream
children will one d
where they will not ...
color of their skin, but by the content
of their character."

Martin Luther King

I have a dream

words to change the world

- MOTIVATE your pupils to write and appreciate poetry.
- INSPIRE them to share their hopes and dreams for the future.
- BOOST awareness of your school's creative ability.
- WORK alongside the National Curriculum or the high level National Qualification Skills.
- Supports the *Every Child Matters - Make a Positive Contribution* outcome.
- Over £7,000 of great prizes for schools and pupils.

"When I was out there I was never ever
alone, there was always a team of people
behind me, in mind if not in body."

Lincolnshire
Edited by Claire Tupholme

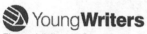 Young**Writers**

First published in Great Britain in 2006 by:
Young Writers
Remus House
Coltsfoot Drive
Peterborough
PE2 9JX
Telephone: 01733 890066
Website: www.youngwriters.co.uk

SB ISBN 1 84602 484 6

Foreword

Imagine a teenager's brain; a fertile yet fragile expanse teeming with ideas, aspirations, questions and emotions. Imagine a classroom full of racing minds, scratching pens writing an endless stream of ideas and thoughts . . .

. . . Imagine your words in print reaching a wider audience. Imagine that maybe, just maybe, your words can make a difference. Strike a chord. Touch a life. Change the world. Imagine no more . . .

'I Have a Dream' is a series of poetry collections written by 11 to 18-year-olds from schools and colleges across the UK and overseas. Pupils were invited to send us their poems using the theme 'I Have a Dream'. Selected entries range from dreams they've experienced to childhood fantasies of stardom and wealth, through inspirational poems of their dreams for a better future and of people who have influenced and inspired their lives.

The series is a snapshot of who and what inspires, influences and enthuses young adults of today. It shows an insight into their hopes, dreams and aspirations of the future and displays how their dreams are an escape from the pressures of today's modern life. Young Writers are proud to present this anthology, which is truly inspired and sure to be an inspiration to all who read it.

Contents

Katie Street (12)	37
Jack Beavis (13)	38
Billie-Jo Baldwin (13)	39
Jodi Wells (12)	40
Jack Cusack (13)	42
Sarah Dickson (13)	43
Martin Haynes (12)	44
Emma Woods (13)	45
Chelsey Johnson (12)	46
Emily Haynes (12)	47
Alex Jones (12)	48
Chris Coe (13)	49
Owain Baxendell (11)	50
Ashley Harris (11)	51
Becky Rudd (12)	52
Rhea Secker (12)	53
Sarah Barnes (11)	54
Leanne Woods (11)	55
Katie Twells (12)	56
Louise Beck (11)	57
Rosie Smith (12)	58
Danielle English (11)	59
Ryan McCready (11)	60
Joseph Thurston (11)	61
Josh Wilson (12)	62
Laurin Dempsey (11)	63
Amy Lee (12)	64
Emma Barclay (11)	65
Adam Taylor (15)	66
Pippa Lambert (15)	67
Alice Britton (14)	68
Chloé Stephens (14)	69
Carl Sheldrick (15)	70
Charlotte Brace (15)	71
Stacey Johnson (15)	72
Jake Clitheroe (15)	73
Alex Baker (11)	74
Warren Beasant (11)	75
Reece Kerry (11)	76
Chloe Pooley (11)	77
Ben Roffe (12)	78
George Steele (11)	79

Aaron Stevens (11)	80
Ben Jex (12)	81
Neil Harrison (12)	82
Terri-Lee Hilton (12)	83
Josh Severn (12)	84
Luke Parish (13)	85
Jake Garner (12)	86
Richard Marriott (13)	87
Rhidian Howarth (12)	88
Jordan Gibb (12)	89
Samantha Bates (13)	90
Paris Hall (12)	91
Lisa Roe (12)	92
Kiene Blake (13)	93
Callum Woods (13)	94
Brittany Kidd (12)	95
Jaime Roberts (13)	96
Charlotte Arnold-Nunn (13)	97
Lacie Devall (13)	98
Laura Dainty (12)	99
Matthew Williams (13)	100
Sharn Taylor (12)	101
Sarah Bettinson (12)	102
Tessa Bustance (12)	103
Natasha Habgood (13)	104
Grant Lester (15)	105
Alex Gibb (15)	106
Aidan Millward (15)	107
Ryan Morris (11)	108
Jordan Jasper (12)	109
Joshua Brown (12)	110
Philip Lewis (14)	111
Sarah Modd (14)	112
Lewis Putman (13)	113
Rosie Warren (13)	114

High Ridge Specialist Sports College

Nathan Dixon (12)	115
Deanne Chadwick-Higgins (12)	116
Lucy Brattan (12)	117
Samantha Loynds (12)	118

Rebecca Hayton (12)   119
Ian Hannaford (11)   120
Nozrul Khan (12)   121
Tahira Akther (12)   122
Luke Willerton (12)   123
Ben White (11)   124
Jordan Noble (12)   125
Calum Haskins (11)   126
William Toyne (12)   127
Hannah Moreton (12)   128
Najma Akther (12)   129
Kate Drury (12)   130
Georgina Elby (11)   131
Jake Smith (11)   132
Afsana Begum (12)   133
Alice Markham (12)   134
Hollie Melton (12)   135
Thomas Doleman (12)   136
Bethany Fisher (11)   137
Nicole Gadd (12)   138
Zoe-Marie Milligan (12)   140
Bradley Reeve (12)   141
Mousumi Choudhury (12)   142
Adam Catley (11)   144
Ayesha Begum (13)   145
Gemma Atterby (12)   146
Nicholas Hutchinson (12)   147
Rebekah Hirst (12)   148
Jemma Reid (12)   149
Jason Stephenson (12)   150
Cátia Vaz (13)   151
Louis Finch (13)   152
Jordan Grace (12)   153
Hayley Houldridge (13)   154

King's School
Adam Cunningham (12)   155
Richard Baker (17)   156

Middlefield School

Queen Elizabeth's Grammar School

The Humberston School

Vale of Ancholme Technology College

Western Technology School

The Poems

I Have A Dream

I have a dream that one day
I will stop animal cruelty,
All animals would have respect,
No dog or cat would be afraid
Of anyone or anything.

All animals would be treated *fairly*.

Gemma Sinfield (12)
Casterton Community College

Perfect World

Bling! Bling! Let the world sing,
Pink! Pink! Let the world think,
Poverty no more.

Ring! Ring! Do your own thing!
Stand up against war!

Natalie Durrant (13)
Casterton Community College

I Wish People Wouldn't Smoke

Smoking kills you,
It kills the people around you,
It makes you high
And then you will die.
Instead of buying cigarettes
You can buy some Nicorette,
You will save a bunch of money
And will save your life.
Then your fingers go yellow
And your teeth black
And they're full of plaque.

Smoking kills you,
You will be addicted
And then you will be predicted.
You will die
And the people around you will cry.
You won't see your kids grow up
Because you will be in six feet of muck.
Remember don't smoke
Or you will choke.

Holand Couzens (13)
Casterton Community College

Why? Why? Why?

Animals dream,
They dream of a healthy life
But their dreams are destroyed
By a scientist who kills them in experiments
Just to study changes.
Why? Why?

Animals test new painkillers,
Which makes them react and die.
Why? Why?
Rabbits turn blind,
Monkeys get affected through cuts.
Why? Why?

Fur is shaved off, still the animals are cut open,
Why? Why?
Muscle is hacked off dogs' thighs.
Why? Why?

Animals dream too,
But their dreams are destroyed
By people who don't care.
Why? Why? Why?

Megan Hooper (12)
Casterton Community College

Animal Testing

What do you think animal testing is?
Well I'll tell you.
We all want to save animals from
Not being able to have a life.
How do you feel?
We all want to stop animal testing,
What can we do?
We can stop animal testing!
How many animals
Do you think die every day?

Are you an animal?
How would you feel?
Every day being injected
By something horrible,
Or horrible way of getting into your body.
How do you feel?
We could stop all this
By saying no, no, no!
So come with us and stop it,
To see all the happy faces.

So, if you help us,
You will help animals.
We can stop animal testing
By helping them.
If we all get together,
We will be a lot stronger.
There are a lot of animals
Which get killed every day.
So let's start helping
To stop animal testing.

Olivia Wilmer (12)
Casterton Community College

My Vision Of A Perfect World

My vision of a perfect world would be . . .
Where no one argues,
Families stay together,
No one dies of illness or at a young age.

My vision of a perfect world would be . . .
The end of war,
The end of fighting between others,
No fighting between religions.

Daniel Green (12)
Cast7erton Community College

Maybe One Day

(Protest song on pollution and recycling)

Maybe one day
I will breathe fresh air,
Knowing it will not happen
Is something I hate.

Maybe one day
I will never see rubbish on the floor,
You will destroy the Earth,
That's something I hate.

Maybe one day
I will see the paths clear,
Not dirty and littered,
That's something I hate.

Maybe one day
When you breathe
It won't lead to death,
That's something I hate.

Maybe one day
The roads will be clean
And the air will be clear,
Now that's something I like.

Ben Lewis (13)
Casterton Community College

I Wish, I Wish, I Wish

I wish that whenever I step out the classroom
I'm not being followed or watched.

I wish that whenever I enter the boys toilet
They won't be there.

I wish that whenever I walk out to the playground
I'm not being stared at or given a dirty look.

I wish that whenever I have PE my school clothes
Don't get hidden or ripped.

I wish that whenever I leave my school
They won't be standing there by the gates.

I wish that whenever I walk out my house
I'm not being waited for at the bottom of the road.

I wish that whenever I wake up I don't
Have to worry about the future.

I wish that whenever I go to sleep
I don't have bad dreams.

I wish that whenever I'm scared
My mum and dad are with me.

I wish I had friends who protected me
When I needed it most.

I wish . . .
I wish . . .
I wish . . .

Edward Grys (13)
Casterton Community College

I Have A Wish!

How many people must you see
Die of cancer
Before you stop smoking?
Every year around 114,000 smokers die.
I have a wish that nobody smoked,
People stop smoking today!

How many people must you see
Getting rushed into hospital,
Unable to breathe?
More than 80% of smokers take
up the habit as teenagers.
I have a wish that smoking was banned!

How many people must you see
Inhale this poisonous smoke,
Sending their lungs black?
You could be breathing in this smoke.
You can't come out of a pub without smelling of smoke!
I have a wish that everyone that
Smokes would stop!

Hannah Johnson (13)
Casterton Community College

I Have A Dream . . .

I have a dream, a beautiful dream,
With flowers, trees and bushes.
One filled with colours that fill the sky,
One where I can go up and fly.

Surrounded by animals,
Bunnies, birds and deer.
In this dream I have no fears,
I have nothing to be afraid of.

No violence,
No crime.
My dream is calm
And there is no harm.
If you want to enter my dream, please do!

Sarah Yardley (12)
Casterton Community College

A Dream

I have a dream that world differences
will be sorted and that leaders will
lead their countries well.

I have a dream that all homeless
people will be helped and all be
found homes and food.

I have a dream that the world will
sort out all differences and people
will abandon all hate.

I have a dream that leaders should
concentrate on people that need money
and food not war.

I have a dream that all of these
dreams will come true and the
world will be great and at peace.

Rosie Barker
Casterton Community College

I Had A Dream

I had a dream,
I had a dream that others would take care of each other,
That people would take care of animals.

I had a dream,
I had a dream the inequalities in the world would be settled,
That litter would not be dropped.

I had a dream,
I had a dream that people would recycle
And not kill the very things that keep us alive,
That we would stop pollution.

I *have* a dream.

Emily Rowbotham (13)
Casterton Community College

No War, No Riots

I have a dream that one day the world will have peace and quiet,
No war with people who die,
No war with people who cry,
No riots with fire,
No riots with bullets.

One day there will be peace,
I hope that is true.
One day there will be quiet,
I hope that is true.
I mean no war, no riots,
Nothing to hurt people in all different ways.

I have a dream that one day the world will have peace and quiet,
No war with people who die,
No war with people who cry,
No riots with fire,
No riots with bullets.

One day there will be a riot where people will die,
But hopefully there will be a clear sky
With no trouble in the world.
One day there will be a war where people will die,
But hopefully there will be a clear sky
With no trouble in the world.

I have a dream that one day the world will have peace and quiet,
No war with people who die,
No war with people who cry,
No riots with fire,
No riots with bullets.

One day if this dream does not come true
There may not be me any longer.

Jake Richardson (12)
Casterton Community College

I Have A Dream

I have a dream, a dream of peace,
A dream of hope that all wars will cease.

I have a dream, of being set free,
Set free like a bird, to fly over the sea.

I have a dream, that everyone on this Earth,
Can speak their mind, right from their birth.

I have a dream, where black and white,
Can come together and finally unite.

Dreams, dreams are powerful things,
But it's up to the people what peace and hope brings.

At the end of the day, we're all the same,
Playing the difficult, hard life game.

Adam Purcell (12)
Casterton Community College

I Have A Dream

I have a dream, a dream of hope,
A dream in which everyone can pray and be forgiven of their sins.

I have a dream, for freedom of everyone,
In every country of every city, of every town.

I have a dream for racism not to happen,
No name calling, bullying or acts of terrorism.

I have a dream for all this to happen,
In years to come,
To be cut out,
For it all to come to an end!

An end to this would mean a lot,
An end to poverty,
To ensure equality
In every part of the world!

Jacob McClarnon (12)
Casterton Community College

Cancer

I have a dream that cancer
Could have a cure,
A lot more people
Could be safe for sure!
Friends and family
No longer have to weep,
And at last the deaths
Can at least sleep in peace!
Wouldn't it be nice
To live in a world,
Where cancer had a cure?
I have a dream
That cancer will kill no more.

Kayleigh Myles (14)
George Farmer Technology & Language College

The Bullies Dream . . .

I have a dream that one day
Schools will be peaceful,
Flowers will flourish with kindness,
The heartbreak in the world will be gone,
That's my dream.

I have a dream that one day
Life will be happier,
Those children will stand up and speak up
In times of trouble,
That's my dream.

I have a dream that one day
The streets will be quiet,
Those gangs will find friends and happiness
In times of worry,
That's my dream.

My dream
Should change the world,
People should have lives again,
Why this dream?

Help those children stand up and speak up,
This dream is a lifetime of love.

Jessica Sauntson (14)
George Farmer Technology & Language College

Hungry People

People starving
With an empty bowl
People hungry
But with a good soul.

We've got lots of water
They haven't got a sip
We've got houses
They live on a tip.

We've got technology
They die every day
We've got the medicine
But we still want the pay.

We've got lots of money
But we spend it on booze
They've got no money
Not even a pair of shoes.

We think it's cruel
You make us come to school
They all need
A very good school.

Toby Holliday (14)
George Farmer Technology & Language College

A Hope For Tomorrow

A hope for tomorrow,
That someone can walk down the road undisturbed,
Regardless of markings of sorrow,
A hope for tomorrow.

When different is synonymous to normal,
A hope for tomorrow,
When you can be who you want to be,
Without need to artificial characteristics borrow.

When you know that you are as free as a river,
A fantasy of the future,
Rushing through a forest of fear, and nothing can harm you,
Strength and determination sutured.

Breaking down the barriers in your path,
A fantasy of the future,
That peace and unity stand strong,
Shut the wide open door of failure forever.

That bullies flee before a wall of unbreakable emotion,
A promise for tomorrow,
A thing you can change,
A hope in your hands.

David Tully (13)
George Farmer Technology & Language College

I Have A Dream . . .

Bring back the thirties,
Or shall I say the flirties!
They didn't care about looks, clothes and hot pants,
You just boogied on down and danced!

It was stripes that were the biggest thing out,
But they didn't know what they looked like, no doubt!
They just waltzed in, in their platform shoes,
And gobbled down the booze!

They boogied all night to rock 'n' roll
Wandering around with a cheeky stroll!
Thinking they were the next Austin Powers,
The teenagers staying out for hours!

Why can't we be like this?
The days when life was so bliss!
I have a dream
And this is it!

Laura Wright (14)
George Farmer Technology & Language College

I Have A Vision

I have a vision
That prisons do not exist,
As crime is an unknown word.

I have a vision
Of no fighting or hate,
And that death only occurs in old age.

I have a vision
That everybody accepts each other,
For the person they naturally are.

I have a vision
That has not yet been discovered
And that everybody had a little love and hope.

Heatha Cross (13)
George Farmer Technology & Language College

I Wish That One Day

I wish that one day
All animals will be cared for,
Having loving owners
And be part of a family.

That no animals will be abused,
Mistreated, starved or abandoned,
A tiny kitten, dumped, kicked,
A huge horse, neglected, skin and bones.

A long snake, cramped, restricted,
A playful dog, sad, lonely,
A miniature hamster, parched, hungry,
A fluffy rabbit, fur matted, teeth overgrown.

No need to have animal sanctuaries,
Or to put down mistreated animals,
If they are ill or nobody wants them,
As I wish all animals will have a caring home.

Jemma Smith **(13)**
George Farmer Technology & Language College

I Have A Dream

I have a dream
That bullying shall be stopped.

I have a dream
Kids shall not live in fear.

I have a dream
That kids shall not be judged by what they look like.

I have a dream
That kids will not have to feel emotional pain.

I have a dream
Bullies shall be punished for what they do.

I have a dream
Bullying shall be a thing of the past.

Joe Johnson (14)
George Farmer Technology & Language College

A Dream Of No Bullying

I have a dream,
No more weeping children.
I have a dream,
A content playground.

I have a dream,
That frowns turn to smiles.
I have a dream,
That bullying is dead.

I have a dream,
We all walk hand in hand.
I have a dream
All around the world.

Bethanie Eldridge (14)
George Farmer Technology & Language College

I Have A Dream

I have a dream
There will be no more pain.

I have a dream
Nobody would suffer.

I have a dream
Everybody would be cured.

I have a dream
Everybody would be equal.

I have a dream
Nobody would be left out.

Lewis Warner (13)
George Farmer Technology & Language College

I Have A Dream

I have a dream
That the whole world was at peace.
I have a dream
That there was no war or terrorism.
I have a dream
That all races were treated as equals.
I have a dream
That everyone had equal rights.
I have a dream
That smoking was banned.
I have a dream
That there is no abuse.
I have a dream,
I have a dream
That everyone is happy!

Jamie Gilbertson (13)
George Farmer Technology & Language College

I Have A Dream

I have a dream
Everyone can live happily and peacefully,
But the world gets filed with dark clouds,
Full of violence,
Hatred and anger.

I have a dream
This darkness could leave,
Never return.
I have a dream that when this happens
We will be happy and cheerful,
We can be free to live.

But bad things do happen and that dream gets shattered for now
And we become distressed
Which leads to mad behaviour by us all.
I have a dream that this can change,
I have a dream.

Zen Severn (14)
George Farmer Technology & Language College

I Dream For Peace

I have a dream
That one day there will be peace,
No war or violence,
A pleasant atmosphere in the world.

I have a dream
There will be no hostility,
No slaughter, no loathing,
No burglaries and even no thieving.

I have a dream
People will love instead of hate,
There will be no quarrelling
And people will get on.

I have a dream
People will get on with their lives,
If they can't do anything to help people,
Then leave them alone.

I have a dream
I would love it to come true,
Let's have peace in the world,
But after all it's only a dream.

David Stubley (14)
George Farmer Technology & Language College

I Wish

I wish for peace,
For everyone to be safe,
Wherever they went,
Whatever they did.

I wish for peace
All over the world,
In every country,
On every planet.

I wish for peace,
With no fighting
And no war,
With happiness spread
Throughout the universe.

I wish for peace,
No bullying,
No name-calling,
No murder.

Doesn't it seem like a nice place?
Everything perfect.
You can make it happen.
You can make a difference.
I wish for peace.

Daniel Vale (13)
George Farmer Technology & Language College

My Dream

I have a dream
That no one was ever harmed
And hospitals were never used,
Never called for.

I have a dream
That animal cruelty would end
And the RSPCA was never used,
Never called for.

I have a dream
That crime would end
And police were never used,
Never called for.

I have a dream
That dreams all come true
And nightmares are never dreamt of,
Never asked for.

Even some dreams are stretched too far,
Sometimes out of reach,
But never stop dreaming.

Kirsty Stevens (13)
George Farmer Technology & Language College

The World Without Crime

A world without crime
Is a world full of amity.
It's about time
Crime should diminish.

Robbery and abuse,
Murder and theft,
Always on the news,
There's not a lot left.

People out there don't deserve it,
It's unfair for them, having to endure,
People who did it should recommit,
Together as one,
We can be together.

The time has arrived,
This madness stops,
A great relief for some,
No need for cops.

Hayley Maloney (14)
George Farmer Technology & Language College

Should It Be A Dream?

I have a dream,
Where no one should suffer,
Children don't wait for death to come and find them,
Why should it be a dream?

I have a dream,
Should people be afraid
To leave their house at night
Fearing what may happen round the corner?
Why should it be a dream?

I have a dream,
Where nobody dies because of his or her race,
Black or white, everybody is the same
Working together in the world,
Why should it be a dream?

I have a dream
Where cancer is no longer a threat,
People will not have to say goodbye
To loved ones anymore young or old,
Why should it be a dream?

I have a dream
Where hearts are never broken
Due to dying love for one another,
People will have forever happiness,
Why should it be a dream?

I have a dream
Where the human race isn't waiting
For global warming to happen,
The human race will never die,
Why should it be a dream?

Sam Broome (13)
George Farmer Technology & Language College

I Believe

I believe
That black people should be treated equally.
I believe
That white people are no better than black people.
I believe
Everyone should have equal rights.
I believe
That racism should be stopped.
I believe
That everyone is equal.
I believe
That dreams come true.
I believe
I had this dream,
Seeing is believing.
I believe
Everyone can be happy.
I believe
That racism should be stopped.

Kathryn Rackham
George Farmer Technology & Language College

Touch The Stars

I had a dream
And you were there,
I had a dream
Where no one stared,
I had a dream
It seems quite far,
I had a dream
To touch the stars.

I had a dream
To help the races,
I had a dream
To take in paces,
I had a dream
It seems quite far,
I had a dream
To touch the stars.

I had a dream
To stop the hunger,
I had a dream
To make people stronger,
I had a dream
It seems quite far,
I had a dream
To touch the stars.

I had a dream
To stop all evil,
I had a dream
To help the people,
I had a dream
It seems quite far,
I had a dream
It's not too far.

Barbara Bearman (13)
George Farmer Technology & Language College

I Have A Dream Tonight

I am falling asleep,
I hear the clock chime midnight,
I'm drifting into a world of dreams,
But what should I dream tonight?

I could dream about animal welfare,
Why can't they all be set free?
Is it true that they are tested
Just to help people like me?

I could dream about countries
And how I wish I could stop war,
Because fighting and blowing other people up
Should be against the law.

Maybe I could dream about bullying,
Why can't racism stop?
And as for people being called names,
Why can't the number of them drop?

So I'm having a dream tonight,
I've had a dream to stop the bad,
But is this the best dream
I have ever had?

Holly Davis (13)
George Farmer Technology & Language College

If I Were In Charge

If I were in charge
This world would be different,
There would be no war,
Discrimination
Or poverty,
If I were in charge.

If I were in charge
Prisons wouldn't be hotels
And crime really wouldn't pay,
Animals wouldn't be tested on,
Criminals would,
If I were in charge.

If I were in charge
I'd get rid of Mugabwe,
I'd take all his money,
I'd put it where it belongs
And prevent future poverty,
If I were in charge.

If I were in charge
I'd stop all hatred,
I'd stop all terrorism
And I'd stop all abuse,
If I were in charge.

Allan Taylor (13)
George Farmer Technology & Language College

Us, We Together

Love goes deeper than skin,
Friendship is thicker than blood,
Look past appearance, clothes, hair,
And look for the person inside.

Blacks with whites,
Together we stand,
Our world, one big country,
Everyone counts. Everyone is equal.

Don't kill. Don't murder
Because he is you,
We are all one
And together we are God.

We control the Earth,
We make it spin,
No wars, no hate,
Just equal love.
Not me and not I,
Just us, we together.

Katie Street (12)
George Farmer Technology & Language College

Reality

This is my dream,
Now where to start.
How about war,
Murders and crime.

This is my dream,
No prisons, more criminals,
More bombs, more fear,
More fights, more deaths.

This is my dream,
Terrorism on the rise,
More racism every day,
What a horrible world we live in.

Apart from, this is not my dream,
This is close to reality.

Jack Beavis (13)
George Farmer Technology & Language College

I Have A Dream

I have a dream
About all people.
I have a dream
On our colour.
I have a dream
On how we talk.
I have a dream
On how we look.
I have a dream
About the world.
I have a dream
On nice places.
I have a dream
About me and everyone.

Billie-Jo Baldwin (13)
George Farmer Technology & Language College

The Dreams Of A Fashion Model

I will show you my dreams,
Show you secrets and surprises,
So far, far away the seem,
Horses flying towards the moon,
Being a fairy-tale ninja pixie,
Hopefully I won't wake up soon.

Here I am a fashion model
Looking totally splendid.
Now I am an actor
Just like I intended,
Whizzing around a marble floor,
I wish I could dance for evermore.

Blousey, Titania and Juliet too,
What's the next part I will do?
Maybe it might be Cinderella,
Slave girl who loses her shoe.
Now the parts are sailing through
At Embassy, Hollywood, London too,
I wonder, what's the next dream I'll go to.

I open the doors, peer through the window,
Seems like I'm spinning the wheel of fortune.
The dream is here,
This time tomorrow, maybe soon
I could be sailing in a hot air balloon,
Drifting above snow-white mountains,
Possibly a sphinx and great sand dunes.

Can I be serious? Yes I can,
The population is eating up our world,
Its great big arms smothered around us,
Our trees can't breathe.
The ozone's thinning,
No one's to blame, but us.
We might not like to see the world,
The world will flood, killing everything, even us!

Now I have shown you my dreams and wishes,
Some are interesting, some too extreme,
Some are weird, some are stupid,
But they're mine and they're supreme!

Jodi Wells (12)
George Farmer Technology & Language College

To Change

I have a dream
To change the world
And to make it a beautiful thing.

To get rid of racism,
To get rid of terrorism,
To get rid of everything bad.

I have a dream
To see the world
In a different way.

To make everything bad into good,
To make starvation end.

I have a dream.

Jack Cusack (13)
George Farmer Technology & Language College

My Life Is My Dream

Be yourself and others will let you,
Be yourself and others will help you,
Be yourself and others will respect you.

You are who you are, accept it,
You are what you are, respect it,
You are what you feel,
You know it.

Make your life a better place,
Live your life, but don't make a face,
Treat your life the best you can,
Just have fun! You don't need a plan.

We are my dream,
You are my dream,
The world is my dream,
I am my dream,
My life is my dream.

Sarah Dickson (13)
George Farmer Technology & Language College

My Vision

I have a vision, a thought, a dream,
A world of love, safety and kindness,
No wars, battles or guns,
A place without bombs, fear and death.

I have a thought, a dream, a vision,
No racist abuse, no killing or fights,
A world with peace, equal rights and plenty of food,
No animal abuse, taxes or drugs.

I have a dream, a vision, a thought,
No droughts, famines or plagues,
A life without pollution, politicians and soldiers,
A place with light, calm and dreams,
I have a vision, and that is all I have.

Martin Haynes (12)
George Farmer Technology & Language College

I Have A Dream

I have a dream,
A dream about life,
Life may be cruel,
Life may be smart,
But life is my dream.

Emma Woods (13)
George Farmer Technology & Language College

I Wish . . .

I have a dream,
A dream of peace,
Of peace and harmony.
Life with happiness and no war
And people living healthily.
I have a dream!

Chelsey Johnson (12)
George Farmer Technology & Language College

Look After Us

I have a dream
All over the world,
Why can't we
Look after it?
It won't exist
In times to come,
Some bad stuff,
Pollution,
Global warming,
We will not be here
When it happens,
But what about those who will?
They're going to hate it,
It won't be their fault,
It will be ours,
Look after ourselves
And the world around us.

Emily Haynes (12)
George Farmer Technology & Language College

A Dream Takes You Places, It's Up To You To Decide If you Go

I had a dream,
It took me over seas,
It took me over land.
It built me,
It broke me,
It made me who I am today.
I had a dream,
In this dream
I took my family with me,
Three kids,
A girl and two boys.
I took them into a land that was masked,
I tried to work out why it was masked.
I had a dream,
Then I woke up and I didn't understand,
I didn't understand anything that happened.
I took my family on a ride over the sea,
I built my hopes up to create a home,
When I was let down I was broken,
Then I understood,
Understood who I was and why.
I am who I am, no one can judge me until I speak.
I had a dream,
I take it with me and it creates me,
I have a dream.

Alex Jones (12)
George Farmer Technology & Language College

My Family Dream

I miss my dad every day,
Missing all the games we used to play,
Wishing he never went away.

I remember all the good times,
They all are in my mind,
Memories are easy to find.

Sometimes life is bad,
Other times it's sad,
Lots of times I feel glad.

Even though he isn't here,
He doesn't live far, he is near
And to me he'll always be dear.

I wish my dad was here,
I wish my mum was here,
When they are both together
They bring me cheer.

Chris Coe (13)
George Farmer Technology & Language College

Wishes

Mother Teresa,
India's feeder.
I need to explain
Again and again.

Martin Luther King
Eliminated the racism thing.
But it still exists
And so I persist.

Kurt Cobain,
Nirvana's back again.
His lyrics made sense,
But they ignore it, they're just dense.

Martin Luther King,
Me again with that racist thing.
It's gone now
But I say how?

Owain Baxendell (11)
George Farmer Technology & Language College

I Have A Vision

I have a vision to make a business as a car mechanic,
Open it to the world,
To design new car components
For the world to see.

I want to become something no one else is,
But it's gonna be hard,
I've got to work hard.

I wish the world was less polluted
And people stopped wheel spinning,
And if people had cleaner engines
It would be a better world.

I want to become something no one else is,
But it's gonna be hard,
I've got to work hard.

Ashley Harris (11)
George Farmer Technology & Language College

That's My Goal

I have a goal to stop all wars,
To let it out and slam the doors,
I wish I knew a cure,
So everything was pure.

I have a goal to help the poor
And maybe be a citizen of law,
I wish that animals could hold out their paws,
So that I could heal all their sores
And that's my goal!

Becky Rudd (12)
George Farmer Technology & Language College

I Have A Dream

I'd like racism and bullying to stop
And friendship to go straight to the top,
Animal cruelty and animal testing,
The world would be better with what I'm suggesting.

I'd personally like to be on TV
And find laughter for you and me,
I'd like to go to vet school and have a nice house,
With bullying and name calling I'd be quiet as a mouse.

Rhea Secker (12)
George Farmer Technology & Language College

My Dreamworld

Sing for the poor,
To help the world,
That's what happens in my dreamworld.
People like the way I sing.

Health is important so people don't die,
That's my dreamworld,
Singing to help problems.

People love other people,
That's what makes the world go round,
That's my dreamworld.

Why not help children get homes,
Like Sarah's children's home,
I wish, I hope.

Sarah Barnes (11)
George Farmer Technology & Language College

I Have A Dream . . .

Help me raise money for cancer,
Buy the special bands
And support me being a special dancer
So I can use my hands.

I have a dream to protect my family,
To learn how to defend,
To know where I'm gonna stand
And to protect my friend.

I want some money
When I am older,
To help my friends and family
To keep rich and pure.

Leanne Woods (11)
George Farmer Technology & Language College

The World Supreme

Times like now
I need a friend,
My dream it is
To help, defend.

Sharing qualities
To become something,
I want to earn some amazing dosh
To help me buy some bling.

Dreams are like friends,
They stick with you, forever,
They glimmer like diamonds
Even in bad weather.

I'll be amazed
If nature is good,
Give them a treat
Of great tasty food.

Oh come to me
My precious dream,
I need to see
The world supreme.

Katie Twells (12)
George Farmer Technology & Language College

Dreams Are Life

Dreams are important to me,
Not only for life but for love.

Dreams for me would be,
To be happy and to have someone love me.

Dreams are ambitions, visions or information,
Like climbing Mount Everest, to go to Africa
and Australia and to stop poverty.

Dreams are wishes and hopes,
Hoping a puppy will love you,
Wishing a dog would live again.

Dreams are like pirates,
Stealing ideas from your head,
Taking and giving confidence.

Dreams are like friends,
There when you need them
And reliable most of the time.

We need dreams,
They are important.

Louise Beck (11)
George Farmer Technology & Language College

My Dream Is To Be . . .

A pro' horse rider
And for no sexual abuse,
This would just be great.

I really like sports,
But I enjoy horse riding,
But I could do both.

I would like the world
To be loving and caring,
So we'll be happy.

My other dream is,
For school to be much more fun,
And for there to be no homework.

Rosie Smith (12)
George Farmer Technology & Language College

Some People Are Different

My dream is to be in . . .
A world with no abuse
Especially to animals
And little children too!

I want to go to university
And get a fantastic job,
Move into a big house
And don't have to pay the bills!

No blind or deaf people
With cancer which can kill,
No arguments or shouting
Or nasty, horrible diseases!

Danielle English (11)
George Farmer Technology & Language College

Dreams Can Change Reality

A man walks down an empty street,
His white robe whistling in the breeze,
The chilling wind moaning and following him at every turn,
A ghost town lies ahead,
Then he sees his loving wife and children,
As pale as his bright robes,
They lay there awake,
But with no air in their lifeless bodies,
'I love you,' he whispers under his breath,
Then as he looks around,
More bodies lay about.
A black cloud hangs over the city,
A cloud of shame,
But looking at the future,
It can all change.
A man walks down a crowded street . . .

Ryan McCready (11)
George Farmer Technology & Language College

My Dream

No people dying,
No more people lying.

More cancer cure,
Give them water that is pure.

Let there be no more fighting,
Or God will start smiting the fighting.

I hope racism will stop,
Everyone is welcome at our shop.

Joseph Thurston (11)
George Farmer Technology & Language College

I Hope

I hope that racism would stop,
I hope every family could buy some pop.

I hope we could make poverty history,
I hope tonight everyone would have tea.

I hope we could find a cancer cure,
I hope we could have water that's pure.

I hope we can have a world with no war,
I hope we can finally shut the door.

I hope I can play for a semi-pro team,
I hope if I do I would shine up and gleam.

Josh Wilson (12)
George Farmer Technology & Language College

Children Are The Same!

My dream is to be,
a teacher to young children,
bringing happiness.

Giving them support,
even if they are disabled,
children are the same.

So they are different,
they could be deaf or blind,
I don't really care.

All I want to do,
is bring them happiness
and give them courage.

Teaching them great things,
giving them great pleasure,
children are the same!

Laurin Dempsey (11)
George Farmer Technology & Language College

I Wish!

I wish racism would stop
And robbing at the shop.
People would be kind
And stop messing with your mind.
The world would be clean
And people wouldn't be mean.
I wish!

Kidnapping would stop,
People wouldn't be shot.
Nobody without a home,
So people wouldn't moan.
I'm a doctor when I'm older,
People would be bolder,
I wish!

Amy Lee (12)
George Farmer Technology & Language College

Sweet Dreams . . .

I have a dream to end all wars
And maybe to enforce new laws.
I wish that there was a cure,
So that cancer would be here no more.

I have a dream to be able to help and cure,
All the people that are rather poor.
I wish that there was no more crime
And this will happen before the end of time.

I have a dream that all colours could come together
And be friends forever.
I wish that people wouldn't be so cruel
To anyone that is small.

Ahh, sweet dreams.

Emma Barclay (11)
George Farmer Technology & Language College

I Have A Dream Of Peace, I Have A Dream

I have a dream,
I dream of green grass,
Clean air and the sound of laughter,
I dream of peace.

I have a dream,
I dream of equality,
The removal of terrorism and fear,
I dream of peace.

I have a dream,
I dream of repairing the damage we've done,
Healing old wounds and helping each other,
I dream of peace.

I have a dream,
I dream of freedom for all,
Loyalty and prosperity,
I dream of peace.

The wounds we make, the chances we take, the words we speak,
The fights we start and the actions we take,
They are not the stuff of destiny, dreams are . . .

I dream,
Of peace.

Adam Taylor (15)
George Farmer Technology & Language College

War Beholds The World

I have a dream
A star in the night sky,
War beholds the world
I look upon the war-torn fields
The sound of silence pains my ears
Stone coffins for the crowd of the forgotten appear
Are we still in fear?

Could the silence possibly be different
Or could I make it different?
I have a dream
It's been ripped at the seams
But it's still a dream
Reality?
It could be.

Pippa Lambert (15)
George Farmer Technology & Language College

Silent Sufferers

When I was little I had a dream,
I dreamt I grew up in a normal family,
That dream didn't come true,
That dream didn't come true for a lot of people.

Abused by loved ones,
Families torn apart by violence,
It's not a stranger,
It's not in the cities,
It's in the place you call your home.

No one wants to live like this,
In fear or terror,
So let's stop it,
Let the dream come true,
It didn't for me,
But let it come true to the sufferers in silence.

Alice Britton (14)
George Farmer Technology & Language College

Suffering Children

Same four walls and nothing to do
It's more like jail,
I longed so much to do the things
I'd never been allowed to do before,
I said it didn't matter
I was just abused every day,
But deep down inside
I was afraid, upset, hurt and bruised.
I said I didn't care for things
Like food, water and such,
I hadn't had any for days on end
Anything would have done,
I couldn't let my life pass by like this,
I couldn't live like this forever.

If I had a dream, it would be to stop child cruelty,
It's horrible, nasty and no child should have to go through it,
Through the abuse.
Most of the time people only do it because they are
Stress and angry,
But why take it out on your children?
It's a nasty offence,
You should stop now before it's too late!
If I had a dream, it would be for abused children
To lead a joyful and happy life
And not think that every time they move
They're going to get hurt!

Chloé Stephens (14)
George Farmer Technology & Language College

Hope

I have a dream of what the future may be
A better place for you and me
Where hunger and poverty are a thing of the past
Where hate is gone and only love holds fast

I have a dream of what the future may be
The sick are healed and the blind can see
The deaf can hear and all pain is gone
All people unite and the world is one

I have a dream of the future of what, when and how
Tomorrow's the future so let's start now.

Carl Sheldrick (15)
George Farmer Technology & Language College

Mysterious Cloud

The touch of a single tulip
Way out in a field.
The atmosphere
Is damp out here
As I sit on the old wooden bench.

In a few years time,
Where's the tulip?
Crushed on the ground!
I hear the wrong sound,
Cars and people chatting.

I turn my head,
I look around,
There it is!
That different sound!

There's no sky!
Why?
But a grey cloud lurking.

Ugly grey buildings,
No green, yellow, red, blue.
All dismantled
But who?

No tulips, grass or trees,
No wildlife, sand or seas,
Just ugly little buildings
And that stupid, polluted cloud.

That cloud has got to go,
That cloud has got to fly,
I've called that cloud pollution
Now it's time to say goodbye.

Charlotte Brace (15)
George Farmer Technology & Language College

A Better Place

The world would be a better place,
You could have a smile upon your face,
No one would be down,
So there's no need for a frown.

No more cruelty,
You will see,
What a better place
The world would be.

No more anger,
No more war,
No more need for the law.

This is my dream,
I hope you can see,
What a better place the world could be!

Stacey Johnson (15)
George Farmer Technology & Language College

A Dream To Live

I have a dream
Of war to stop
And hatred and love
To unite as one
I have a dream
Of cancer and death
To be cured at last
Smokers just bring death ever closer
I have a dream
Of racism to end
The colour of your skin
Is not your fault

I have a dream
To make my dream
Reality.

Jake Clitheroe (15)
George Farmer Technology & Language College

Dream Poem

P oor people
O ld people
V ery, very sick people
E veryone sad
R abid animals
T elevision adverts -
Y ou could be helpful and save money for them.

Alex Baker (11)
George Farmer Technology & Language College

War

War, war, war,
It makes people poor.
Please no more,
War, war, war.

Pain, pain, pain,
It makes people insane.
Please stop it again,
Pain, pain, pain.

Tears, tears, tears,
It makes people fear,
As war is so near,
Tears, tears, tears.

Warren Beasant (11)
George Farmer Technology & Language College

Recycling

R ecycle all your rubbish
E expect to help recycle
C ans, bottles in the bins
Y ou need to be helpful
C ome and see what's happened
L ong time to think about this
I t is now very hard
N ot doing much at all
G o and clean your junk!

Reece Kerry (11)
George Farmer Technology & Language College

We Are All Equal

Whether you are black or white -
We are all equal!

Blacks and whites commit murder -
We are all equal!

We can stop racism -
We are all equal!

We need to stop all racism -
We are all equal!

We need to speak out -
We are all equal!

Everybody deserves his or her say -
We are all equal!

We should all listen -
We are all equal!

We are all equal!
We are all equal!

Chloe Pooley (11)
George Farmer Technology & Language College

Imagine

Imagine not being fed.
Imagine living with a cruel owner.
Imagine being on he streets,
Because nobody wants you.
That is *animal cruelty*.

Imagine being frightened of your owner.
Imagine being covered in oil that is polluted.
That is *animal cruelty*.

Imagine being rescued.
Imagine being fed.
That is not *animal cruelty*.

Imagine being loved by your owner.
Imagine being stroked.
Imagine having the warmest bed.
That is not *animal cruelty*.

Be kind to your animals!

Ben Roffe (12)
George Farmer Technology & Language College

Wars

W ars are dangerous
A nd people get killed, but
R espect for the people who have to fight
S oon will we learn to end our plight?

George Steele (11)
George Farmer Technology & Language College

We Are Going To Die

G as getting global
L orries loading trash
O bscene amounts of rubbish
B uilding into hills
A re we going to die?
L ight flames burning refuse

W arming up the world
A re we going to die?
R ank and rotting piles of garbage
M aking me feel sick
I n a pile, it makes me mad
N ine, nine, nine, emergency
G etting global as we speak . . .

We are going to die.

Aaron Stevens (11)
George Farmer Technology & Language College

My Peaceful Dream

Freedom is a pathway to a person's heart,
As dreams open the trust, faith and desire,
I dream of a world of no hate,
Without racism piercing the soul of belief.

Dishonesty is like a bed of pointy nails,
Burning with pain and itching all over,
I dream of a place without a cold heart,
Yet I come to realise that there is no such thing.

Happiness is the trust in your friends
And sadness is the key to a broken heart,
I dream that people stay together,
Sharing their love like an everlasting flame.

A world without a care is what I dream of,
Where all the bad things are cast away,
I dream of a universe without a big bully,
But a warm, cosy hug and a little kiss goodnight.

Ben Jex (12)
George Farmer Technology & Language College

My Dreamworld

I have a dream
All poverty is gone
All famine has disappeared
That's my dream!

I have a dream
No murders or violent crime
No crime of all kinds
That's my dream!

I have a dream
All countries unite
No wars, no conflicts
That's my dream!

I had a dream
All my dreams had come true
The world was a better place for me and you
That was my dream!

Neil Harrison (12)
George Farmer Technology & Language College

Lands Far Away

My dreams are full of emotions,
They take me to lands far away,
People are no longer angry,
The wars are all at bay.

Rainbows, sunshine and warmth,
It would be the perfect place,
To live and to be happy,
Smiling and laughing, until I wake.

I sometimes take my friends with me,
To this very special land,
They never seem to remember
The fun and play we had.

Then it's time to leave,
That is when I wake up,
Until the next visit,
Deep within my sleep.

Terri-Lee Hilton (12)
George Farmer Technology & Language College

Where I Would Like To Be

I have a dream,
Where the sun will warm us with its beam,
Where everything is nice,
And I can go and get advice.
In my dream is where I would like to be.

I have a dream,
Where colour is not what it seems,
Where people care
And everything is fair.
In my dream is where I would like to be.

I have a dream,
Where we all work as a team,
Where the sun comes out
And nobody would shout
I wish you could see.
In my dream is where I would like to be.

I have a dream,
Where nobody would scream,
And nobody can bleed,
And nobody is in the hands of greed.
My dream is so full of ideas I can't put them all down.

Josh Severn (12)
George Farmer Technology & Language College

Dream Of Hope

Dreams are like the weather,
They change without a care,
One minute, a sassy dream,
The next, a stormy nightmare.

Dreams are like the unknown,
You think it very odd,
But in your dream the unknown happens,
When you tread where others cannot.

Dreams are like people,
They come in different types,
Some tall, some small,
Some old, smoking pipes.

Our world is full of anger,
Full of crying and people that mope,
The sound of gunshots in our ears,
But in my dream, there's hope.

Luke Parish (13)
George Farmer Technology & Language College

Freedom Is Lonely

Freedom is like fire,
It can spread to afar,
But can also burn out like dreams.

Freedom is like water,
It slowly washes away,
But can hit again as a tsunami but this time to stay.

Freedom is like earth,
It is fertile and lets things grow,
But the vicious sun can make it burn down into the ground.

Freedom is like wind,
It brings a nice cool breeze,
But slowly blows away like my dreams.

Jake Garner (12)
George Farmer Technology & Language College

The Hidden Truth

The future is abstract,
No one knows why.
But they come to me for answers,
I'm not psychic but a normal guy.

Why do people think I'm psychic?
I think it's really weird.
But when I make true predictions,
In some places I am feared.

Why is all this happening?
It's really quite confusing.
I'm saying things that are coming true,
And my daughter thinks it's amusing.

I think that I could change the Earth,
With all my future facts.
Like the increasing pollution,
Is melting the polar ice caps.

People think I'm crazy,
But hopefully they will find,
My powers are evolving,
And soon I'll bend their minds.

Richard Marriott (13)
George Farmer Technology & Language College

The Fighter Of Freedom's Chant

The fighter of freedom
Brave and true
Fighting the invasion of anger
Just like you.

Freedom comes to those who fight.
Freedom comes to those who are right.

The fighter of freedom
Do what they should.
Speak out for those who can't,
If only we could.

Freedom comes to those who fight.
Freedom comes to those who are right.

The fighter of freedom
Maybe they're mad.
Fighting for something they do not have.
For freedom in Baghdad.

Freedom comes to those who fight.
Freedom comes to those who are right.

Can you see them
Marching in a line?
All your brothers and sisters dying
And politicians don't mind.

Freedom comes to those who fight
Not to those who might.

Rhidian Howarth (12)
George Farmer Technology & Language College

Caged Dreams

If you aren't free,
Then you are no better,
Than a lion in a zoo.

The lion used to be free,
Roaming across Africa's lands,
Until he got snatched,
Shot, face-down in the sand.

The lion is recovering now,
But the memories
Will never go.

But he dreams of being back
Where he belongs,
Roaming across Africa's lands
Once again he's free,
Because he can dream.

Jordan Gibb (12)
George Farmer Technology & Language College

Dreaming Dreams

Dreams are only made up of what you are thinking,
Dreams are like the seaside,
It will come in then go back out again,
Dreams will come and go.

In my dreams are the most unusual things,
Things not even I understand,
Dreams make you feel free.

The thing about dreams is they will never hurt you,
I had a dream the other night,
About my family and me,
We were rich and had everything,
I wish it was true,
But it doesn't really matter
Because we'll always have each other.

Samantha Bates (13)
George Farmer Technology & Language College

Dreams Are Like The Future

Dreams are like the future,
They're sharp like burning pain,
They turn round every corner,
And point to the right lane.

Dreams are like the future,
They can be smooth and calm,
They fill you up with joy,
Like a priest reading a psalm.

Dreams are like the future,
They change like an icy river,
That's how I lost my mother.

Dreams are like the future,
We hold so very deep,
One day I needed to ask a special person
But still remember you are only just asleep.

Paris Hall (12)
George Farmer Technology & Language College

Freedom In The Present Tense

Dreams are like water.
Can be soft or rough.
Flowing down the stream,
Your mind gets washed away.

In your dreams
You wish and admire
Flaming like a fire
Burning and heart-breaking hot.

Dreams contain different things,
Ambition, fantasy and hope.
Dreams can be good or bad,
Long, short or even angry!

Dreams can be like freedom,
It's sugar to the heart.
Dreams can be in past,
Future or present tense.

Lisa Roe (12)
George Farmer Technology & Language College

Forever Dreams

In my dream
I'm a lost star,
Floating in the sky
Just going afar.

In my dream
I'm a floating river,
But I'm bleeding inside
Like a raw piece of liver.

In my dream
I'm an injured man,
A metal pain shoots through my skin
Feeling like a slaughtered lamb.

In my dream
I'm asleep forever,
When am I going to wake?
A voice inside tells me never.

Kiene Blake (13)
George Farmer Technology & Language College

Dreams And Nightmares

Dreams tell the future,
Nightmares can too.
Both tell you what to do.
If you want to know
Or if you don't
They tell you anyway
Good or bad
Sometimes they tell you things you like
Others tell you things you hate
However
Sometimes,
They tell stories
That you can't
Remember
Or nightmares
That stick with you forever
Wherever
However
Whenever
Dreams and nightmares
Will
Always
Happen!

Callum Woods (13)
George Farmer Technology & Language College

Every Night

Every night,
When the clock hits ten,
My head hits the pillow
And my dreams start then.

Every night,
When the clock hits eleven,
I dream of my childhood,
When I was seven.

Every night,
When the clock hits twelve,
I go to school one day
And I get expelled.

Every night,
When the clock hits one,
I am a teenager,
Oh boy I am glum.

Every night,
When the clock hits two,
I dream I have one baby,
But I end up with two.

Every night,
When the clock hits three,
I look in the mirror
And I am an OAP.

I've awoken from my dream,
I've been to the future,
I shall wait till tonight,
To see whether I go further!

Brittany Kidd (12)
George Farmer Technology & Language College

The Champ

My dream is to win the title,
To be the very best,
I'll fight and fight,
Until I lay to rest.

I will never forget my first fight,
The blood, the sweat, the title in my sight,
The adrenaline rush as my opponent falls down,
Getting me closer to that crown.

My coach he was the very best,
Setting me the hardest test,
To believe in myself,
That I can be the very best.

That next year the championship was mine,
I had worked my way up,
Although it had taken time,
I couldn't believe it - *the title was finally mine.*

Jaime Roberts (13)
George Farmer Technology & Language College

Rainbow Dreams

Dreams are like the rain,
You're feeling really down.
The sun peaks out, the rain grows calm,
The rainbow comes to terms.

Dreams are like a rainbow,
You are feeling a bit better,
But at the end, what is there?
A colourful arch stands before you.

Rainbow dreams have lots of colours,
When you're happy your colour is blue.
The rainbow disappears and so does the rain,
But that doesn't matter, you're happy again.

Rainbow dreams are like life,
All different shades of emotions.
The rain is sadness, but it gets better
The colours are happiness, you are better again.

Charlotte Arnold-Nunn (13)
George Farmer Technology & Language College

Dreams

Dreams are like the sky,
It is always there
But you can never quite grab it.

Dreams are like roses,
They always manage to blossom.

Dreams are like your family,
No matter what, they always expand.

But most of the time
Dreams are nothing more or nothing less,
Than just *dreams!*

Lacie Devall (13)
George Farmer Technology & Language College

In My Dreams

In my dreams I've travelled,
I've travelled far and wide,
I've done many things, I've even skydived.

I've climbed over mountains,
I've lived to tell the tale,
I've met many things, even a giant African snail.

I've smelt many things,
I've tasted some too,
I've heard many sounds like the wild birds' coo.

If only all dreams were all like these,
I would take pictures,
Now dreams, say 'cheese'.

Laura Dainty (12)
George Farmer Technology & Language College

House Of Nightmares

In my house the fiery blaze spread,
The dog started barking noisily in my head,
Looking around waking Mum and Dad,
Losing a family member, everyone is sad.

Now we live just the three of us,
Mourning upon a grave of dust,
The place where our house was once in the past,
Wishing we had got to the other room fast.

It's not very fun all alone in a big house,
But at least I still have my mum and dad,
Their love around but distant from me,
Wishing I was dead instead of he.

Matthew Williams (13)
George Farmer Technology & Language College

Dreams Are Like . . .

Dreams are like stars,
They shine in the night's sky.
If you don't remember them,
They are always in your eyes.

Dreams are like the sky,
You can see but never touch.
They may never come true,
But in them you can forever trust.

Dreams are like the moon,
They shine so bright.
They seem like fantasy in the day,
But seem so real at night.

Sharn Taylor (12)
George Farmer Technology & Language College

Weather Dreams

Dreams
Are like hopes
You want them
To be true.

Dreams
Are like the wind
You can blow
Them away.

Dreams
Are like fire
That dies
In the rain.

Dreams
Can be like the sun
It shines
When you are happy.

They can also
Be like
The weather
Changing every minute.

Sarah Bettinson (12)
George Farmer Technology & Language College

Dreams Of Freedom

Dreams are like water
Calm, rough and pain.

Dreams are like a fire
Dying in the rain.

Some are like the weather
Changing every day.

Some are like hopes
A long way away.

Dreams are full of memories
Sad, happy and true.

Dreams are full of freedom
Whatever is right for you.

Tessa Bustance (12)
George Farmer Technology & Language College

Dreams Are Many Things

Dreams are like butterflies
They flutter in my head
Like whispers of the wind
Or in things I have read.

Dreams are like clouds
They drift in my mind
They take me to places
I otherwise can't find.

Dreams are like rivers
Flowing with happiness
The memories are mine
But you can only guess.

Dreams are like seeds
They take root in my brain
They blossom into lovely things
I'd love to see again.

Natasha Habgood (13)
George Farmer Technology & Language College

Life Of A Rock Star

I have to dream,
So far away.
But if I keep trying,
It'll happen some day.

I'm a rock star,
That's what I'll be.
I'll keep playing that bass
And I'll be history.

I'll grow ma' hair,
All straight 'n' long.
I will look all cool on stage,
While playin' ma' song.

I know I'll die,
Die from ma' drink.
But music's more to me,
So I will have to think.

I'll change the world,
Like Hendrix and Slash.
I know they are better,
But I sure beat The Clash.

Everyone,
Will listen to me,
The OAPs
And kids as young as three.

Love in the air
And some in the sea,
The love of music,
My music made by me.

I have a dream,
So far away.
But if I keep trying,
It'll happen some day.

Grant Lester (15)
George Farmer Technology & Language College

My Dream

I have a dream,
        To be an Olympic runner
I have a dream,
        To make the British squad in 2012.

In the next 20 years let's hope for
        More sponsorship for runners.
In the next 20 years let's hope for
        More government funding for training.

I have a dream,
        To be the one holding the gold medal
I have a dream,
        To grow into a good, strong and healthy man.

Alex Gibb (15)
George Farmer Technology & Language College

Rock Star

Ever since I first picked up a guitar
I dreamed of playing like Slash and Page
20,000 people chanting my band's name
As I step out onto the stage.
I continue my dream to change music
Just like Jimi Hendrix,
But not drowning in sick.
I grab my signature Les Paul
And I play our ballad 'Choices'
Everyone with lighters in their hands
Singing at the tops of their voices.
In just 3 weeks
I'll pick up a Grammy in New York
Beating off talentless wannabes
Like Usher, 50 Cent and Son of Dork.

Aidan Millward (15)
George Farmer Technology & Language College

Starving Children

S cary people who are going to die,
T ragedy is all around.
A round us is a world of disaster.
R unning to get more drink to keep them alive;
V ery little time for the children.
A frica needs more food and drink.
T rying to stay alive for a longer time.
I diots who don't donate for the poor.
O ften eating a little bit, but not enough:
N othing for the poor people.

Ryan Morris (11)
George Farmer Technology & Language College

Drugs

D ealers selling coke,
R uining people's lives.
U gly trade:
G etting bigger.
S hame on them!

Jordan Jasper (12)
George Farmer Technology & Language College

I Have A Vision

I have a vision . . .
A vision to become a computer programmer.
To bring computers to the next generation
And give entertainment for everyone!

Entertainment is fun!
It can be lots of things.
Music, games, videos and the Net are all entertainment!
All together it can be called media!

The Internet is exciting!
Provide access to the Net
Even provide services, chat with other people!
Instant messages to keep in contact with friends.

My vision is to become a computer programmer!
I will have to do well in school
And learn computer languages like . . .
C#, C++, VB.Net and many more.

That is my vision!

Joshua Brown (12)
George Farmer Technology & Language College

My Dream Goal

I really want to score a goal
To make my coach proud
'You can't play,' he says
I think I can
'Let me play, I'll prove it.'
One day I will score
The winning goal!
Around the opposition I will go
Just the keeper left
Me against him
I pull back my foot
Kick
The goalie dives
He's wide
It's in
The crowd is loud
My dream, my moment, my goal!

Philip Lewis (14)
George Farmer Technology & Language College

I Have A Dream

I have a dream of swimming with dolphins
In the blue gleaming sea.
I loved to glide through the water
Before they jump over me.

I dream of being a mermaid swimming in the sea,
So that I can spend all my time with the dolphins
And they will fall in love with me.

I know this dream sounds stupid,
But it's something I have to do
And I am saving all my money
So that I can swim with them soon.

Before I go there's something I must do,
Kiss them one by one and thank them
For making my dream come true.

Sarah Modd (14)
George Farmer Technology & Language College

I Want To Grow Wings

I wanna be a fighter pilot
The best fighter there can be,
I get in my jet, turn on the thrusters
Fly off into battle!

I wanna be a fighter pilot
Nothing else,
I've got that urge to fly about,
I need to fly,
Around in the sky.

The army, the navy,
It's just not for me,
The RAF
That's where I need to be.

Returning to base
I see the horizon,
There they are
I can see them,
They're all waiting for me.

I get back to base
And prepare for weekend leave
And I go for a pint with the lads.

Lewis Putman (13)
George Farmer Technology & Language College

I Have A Dream That One Day . . .

I dream that one day
Equality will develop.
I dream that one day
Colours of skin don't matter.
I dream that one day
Life will be serene.
I dream that one day
Racism will be banished.
I dream that one day
Poverty will vanish.
I dream that one day
There's a cure for cancer.
I wish that my dreams would come true.

Rosie Warren (13)
George Farmer Technology & Language College

I Have A Dream

The people's dignity has been crushed under poverty,
Dying sadly but surely in the pit of death.
I have a dream,
People living in houses, happy,
Alive, not dead,
Sleeping silently,
Not awake on the alert.

I have a dream,
People having jobs, not begging,
Making money,
Having homes,
Having a life.

I have a dream of peace in the world,
No guns,
No weapons,
No war!
Is war good?
Does it get you anywhere?
No!
It only takes you to . . . death.

Nathan Dixon (12)
High Ridge Specialist Sports College

Tears

A tear glistens in a child's eye,
But why should this child ever cry?
'For war,' she said and bowed her head,
'Because of war my dad is dead.'

A hundred days her father fought,
But at the end he'd achieved nought,
We fight for freedom, the hope to be free.
'But where is the freedom?'
This daughter pleads.

'They have the money for guns and weapons,
But needy children, we come second,'
Her heart is broken, 'fighting is bad,'
She quietly mumbled, 'I miss my dad.'

This visit has acted out all of my fears,
I bit my lip to hold back the tears.
She stared straight at me, with eyes of blue
And whispered to me,
'I wish I was you.'

Deanne Chadwick-Higgins (12)
High Ridge Specialist Sports College

I Have A Dream

I have a dream
that the countries of the world
will embrace each other
with love and affection.

I have a dream
that racism is stopped
and everyone is treated equally
and fairly.

I have a dream
that all animals have no fear
of mankind's actions
and can have a safe world to live in.

I have a dream
that the people of the world
come to a decision of justice
and respect towards each other.

I have a dream
that the starving children
are fed the power of opportunity
and choice.

I have a dream . . .

Lucy Brattan (12)
High Ridge Specialist Sports College

I Have A Dream

I have a dream that peace shall finally hush the crying world,
That help shall come to the children who lay in the gutter curled,
That tigers shall be able to run free,
As poachers want to leave them be,
That toucans shall no longer be trapped behind bars,
That the air shall not be polluted by cars,
To rid orphans from their look of fear
And hush up any straying tear.

I have a dream that more people shall stop and think,
For what seems to be the main problem is food and drink,
But you need to look under the cover and at the pages,
To see the real disaster and pain,
It can be as simple as not being paid your wages,
Or hostage situations in which no one gains.

My final dream is that people shall die in their sleep,
For sleep is a peace in itself,
For those who inside are falling apart,
Shall finally learn that you need more than wealth,
And those who tease and bully,
Should first take a look at themselves,
For no one has the right to bully unless they are perfect
And no one's perfect.

Samantha Loynds (12)
High Ridge Specialist Sports College

I Have A Dream

I have a dream that one day
the world will be quiet and free
of all that is bad.

Full of kindness and respect
the world has once shown,
not battles and the murders
people have known.

I have a dream that one day,
all the animals will be free
animals will be running free
through the green lush lands,
not on plates or in our hands.

I have a dream that one day,
nobody will be evil or will bully.
The bullies will be punished
and the well-behaved rewarded
for their kindness to the world.

My final dream is
to stop the hunger in Africa.
No one will go hungry
with illness inches away.
Starving children will fill their tummies
and live another day.

Rebecca Hayton (12)
High Ridge Specialist Sports College

I Have A Dream

I have a dream that the world will be at peace
I have a dream that poverty will be a thing of the past
I have a dream that all diseases will be treated

I have a dream that all weapons will be destroyed
And former enemies will shake hands
Police will have no robberies and murders in hand

I have a dream that food will be given to those in need
All people will have a home
And all children will go to school

I have a dream that science and medicine will be better funded
And treatment for people and animals will be free.

Ian Hannaford (11)
High Ridge Specialist Sports College

I Have A Dream!

I have a dream,
Everybody was treated the same,
Not like garbage,
Dirty and lame,
It doesn't matter if you're black or white,
No more wars and no more fights.

I have a dream,
Poverty would come to an end,
No more starving,
We will have to mend,
Food and water we will give,
To help the poor people thrive and live.

I have a dream,
There was a cure to every disease,
No more crying,
Or suffering or dying,
Millions of people die every day,
Because of diseases that won't go away.

Nozrul Khan (12)
High Ridge Specialist Sports College

I Have A Dream

Peace is my dream for all the world
Clasped in the depths of my thought.
It taunts me every now and then
Even though the restless past has fought.

Peace is my dream for all the world
But first does it exist?
Before I make my decision
Surely no one shall resist.

Peace was my dream for all the world
I wonder why it's happened!
They hurt me so unmercifully
They did it so intentionally.

Yet peace was, still is, my dream
Something I stood up for.
It's something that needs to be fulfilled
It'll continue for evermore.

Peace is my dream for all the world forever!

Tahira Akther (12)
High Ridge Specialist Sports College

I Have A Dream

I hear a child crying,
I see another man dying.

Some people live in poor countries,
Some live in high luxuries.

To prevent infection you need drugs,
But most people don't even own mugs.

People don't have many possessions,
Killers kill because of obsessions.

Something bad could have been
In their childhood they could have seen.

If we work as a team
We can accomplish my dream.

Luke Willerton (12)
High Ridge Specialist Sports College

I Have A Dream

I have a dream that guns will be banned,
Hunger and poverty wiped out from our land,
I have a dream that our world of dismay
Was conquered at last and thrown away.

Illness and dying, it shouldn't be here,
But now it's here, it gives many a tear,
The crying of children, they fight for their life,
On the streets of Baghdad face to face with a knife.

Ben White (11)
High Ridge Specialist Sports College

I Have A Wish

I have a wish for pure world peace,
Every father, son, mother, daughter, grandparent, nephew and niece,
Could go to bed knowing
There is no danger showing.

I have a wish for no world starvation,
They have no food or water in that location,
No cures for diseases,
Not just coughs or sneezes.

I have a wish for no natural disasters,
No more tsunamis, hurricanes as they are all sinister,
They endanger the lives of many
And leave people without a penny.

Jordan Noble (12)
High Ridge Specialist Sports College

I Have A Dream

I have a dream that the whales
could dodge the impales
of the fisherman's nails

I have a dream that the fish
could stay off our dish
how I wish

Why can't they leave them alone?
Disturbing the sea and the foam
taken from their home

They should be a thing we admire
a thing to inspire
not a thing we desire.

Calum Haskins (11)
High Ridge Specialist Sports College

I Have A Dream

I have a dream, a dream that malaria and polio will be cured
and poverty will end
I have a dream, a dream all life can live together forever
and that even just for one minute the world
Thinks of all the men and women that dedicated their whole lives
to the less fortunate.

I have a dream, a dream countries talk arguments over
instead of just fighting, let the Earth choose and not choose for it
I have a dream, a dream the people on this planet will work together
like the ants gathering food for the colony.

I have a dream, a dream that there will be no more racism
because in the end we're all the same no matter what part of the world
we come from
I have a dream, a dream that all crime will be stamped on and crushed
I have a dream, a dream that there will be no more days
like September 11th 2001
I have a dream, a dream that there will be no more terrorism.

I have a dream, a dream of world peace
I have a dream, a dream of Heaven on Earth.

William Toyne (12)
High Ridge Specialist Sports College

I Have A Dream

In a land that is ours,
Filled with the screeches of cars,
A dream is like a precious gem,
Less to us, than it is to them,
'Them' as in the poorest souls,
Who walk the streets
And rest in holes.

Holes that are as empty as our sea,
Where whales used to swim in Galilee,
Oil has destroyed many breeds of fish,
To bring them back is my everlasting wish,
Wishing is like a cosy dream,
Not a nightmare to make you scream,
To see fish swim in freedom once again,
Will begin to ease my wish's pain.

Pain as hollow as our jungles,
That became empty in evil mumbles,
A dream to them, is a dream lost,
As we destroy their homes at a terrible cost,
Endangered circles their every breath,
I have a dream that isn't shadowed with death.

Death is happening beneath our feet,
Is it true that revenge is sweet?
Sweet enough in Iraq,
To earn each soldier a golden plaque?
Dreaming is calm, as is peace,
Carry on dreaming and the wars might cease.

Hannah Moreton (12)
High Ridge Specialist Sports College

I Have A Dream

I have a dream,
for the world to just have peace.
It would be amazing
won't you just love it?
Imagine if everyone thought of the poor,
the people who have no food to spare,
no money to spend,
what if everyone was wealthy in this world?

I have a dream,
of racism not existing.
Everyone would get respect,
no hurt feelings,
just happiness.

I have a dream,
to have the capability of freedom,
to do good things in life,
no bad affecting others,
vandalising stopped,
bullying put to an end.

I have a dream,
to have peace for the rest of all our lives,
I really do have a dream for peace and happiness,
we all can make my dream come true,
let's all believe in ourselves and ask for peace.

Najma Akther (12)
High Ridge Specialist Sports College

They Have A Dream!

I have a dream that animal cruelty will become a thing of the past,
that all endangered species will last and last,
that the lion will get to keep his fur
and we will hear him softly purr.

I have a dream to save them all,
the elephant so big, the mouse so small,
to save them all from a life of pain
would be in itself a fantastic gain.

I have a dream to keep them alive,
to watch them all blissfully thrive,
to save them from a life of dread
where all they want is to fall down dead.

I have a dream, they have one too
now my question is,
do any of you?

Kate Drury (12)
High Ridge Specialist Sports College

I Have A Dream

I have a dream
That one day
Black, white, rich or poor,
One day we will *all* have a say,
In what *we* think is right
And *whatever* people say,
What *we* think is right,
Is *neither* wrong or right,
It's our opinion.

But there is no need to fight about it,
No need at all
And when we call for the doves of peace,
We should smile and rejoice,
Forget our sins and start anew.
Forget colour and anger,
But *remember*
Who we are inside.

If all men were like Martin Luther King,
Then the world would be fit to live in.
If all the women were like Mother Teresa,
All the women would be saints.

I have a dream that should be your dream,
Rid the world of poverty,
Rid the world of racism,
Rid the world of anger,
Let the world shine with peace, love, kindness and *care*.

Georgina Elby (11)
High Ridge Specialist Sports College

I Have A Dream

I have a dream
that everyone in our world is treated the same
not differently,
because they're not the same colour
or they don't speak the same language as us.

I have a dream
that people don't waste their money on sweets or comics
but maybe donate
to places like Asia
who had the tsunami.

I have a dream
that the Third World countries have enough money to build
bigger and stronger houses
which would hold more people
so less would die of being homeless.

I have a dream
that the poorer countries were introduced
to wells with clear drinkable water or games
for all of the children to play with
instead of doing chores all day, every day.

Jake Smith (11)
High Ridge Specialist Sports College

I Have A Dream

I have a dream that some day
life will bring all our dreams
our way,
therefore may our dreams not lay.

I have a dream that some day
everyone can say
hey!

The dreams that we laid may be true, okay.

Afsana Begum (12)
High Ridge Specialist Sports College

I Have A Dream

I have a dream
that some day
we are all able,
able to have our way
and all lives are stable.

I have a dream
that some day
everyone will be friends
and people will be okay,
until the very end.

I have a dream
that some day
some day life will be fine,
friends will be there,
there to stay
and the sun will shine.
I have a dream.

Alice Markham (12)
High Ridge Specialist Sports College

I Have A Dream

I have a dream,
Racism will be a thing of the past,
And that cancer stick will be your last,
Save energy resources,
Live for tomorrow,
Live life in peace,
And not in sorrow.

I have a dream,
Hungry children of Earth shall not exist,
Dealers in drugs will have to resist,
Live for today,
Forgive and forget,
Live your own life,
Live life without regret.

This dream seems so distant,
But it's not that far,
Laugh with the world,
Ha, ha, ha.

Hollie Melton (12)
High Ridge Specialist Sports College

I Have A Dream

I have a dream that the world has peace,
No more war and don't be a beast.
I don't want there to be a World War III,
World War I and II was enough for me.

I have a dream a day won't go by
Without going past an old man and saying hi.
Don't go up to him and nick all his money,
It's not smart, it's not clever and it's definitely not funny.

I have a dream there is no more hunting,
No more dead foxes, this is what I am wanting.
Don't hunt bears, deer, seals or cats,
For mounting on walls or hair for mats.

Thomas Doleman (12)
High Ridge Specialist Sports College

I Have A Dream

I have a dream that
The people of the world were kind,
Papers for banning cruelty were signed,
Everyone got the respect they deserved.
This special world of ours should be preserved.

I have a dream that
The birds were left to fly,
Rays could be seen amongst the clear blue sky,
In our incredible world -
No animals were in danger,
Our friends from the wildlife were beautiful strangers.

I have a dream that
The children learned what they needed to know,
They travelled the places they wanted to go.
Children had as much fun as they could,
As many people believe they should.

I have a dream that
People stood up for their own rights,
All the places of the world were such grateful sights,
I wish our country would flow like a stream,
This is what happened
In my wonderful dream.

Bethany Fisher (11)
High Ridge Specialist Sports College

I Have A Dream

I have a dream
that one day
all animals will stop being killed.
I have a dream
that there will be
no more wars.
I have a dream
that coloured people
will be treated as normal people.
I have a dream
that children
will stop being abused.

Down with poachers,
let animals live.
Down with wars,
no more fighting.
Down with racism,
we're all equal.
Down with abuse,
leave kids alone.

I have a dream
that one day
all gambling will stop.
I have a dream
that one day
bribery will stop.
I have a dream
that one day
all poverty will stop.
I have a dream
that one day
all people will be treated fairly.

Down with gambling,
don't throw your money away.
Down with bribery,
do something to your own accord.
Down with poverty,
let's all afford something.
Down with any inequality,
let's all be treated fairly.

Nicole Gadd (12)
High Ridge Specialist Sports College

I Have A Dream

People use racism as
a cause for destruction,
we use it too much.

I think the world is like
a bright red lipstick,
we use it too much.

The lipstick symbolises blood
and the fact that it shrinks when
we use it too much.

The world, lipstick
what's the difference?
They both end up wasted when
we use it too much.

I have a dream
that people would get along,
help each other then we won't be
using it too much.

Zoe-Marie Milligan (12)
High Ridge Specialist Sports College

I Have A Dream!

I have a dream
I saw a world
without racism
everyone getting along.

I thought this was astonishing
I thought, put it to the test
to stop racism
around the world.

I gather the people
in a large space
to protest against racism
and live in peace.

Not allowed to be together
by order of the residents.
How can we make the world amazing?
To stop people being belligerent.

Black people getting agitated
White people being belligerent
Martin Luther King shot down
and racism against the law.

Wow, the dream is over.

Bradley Reeve (12)
High Ridge Specialist Sports College

I Have A Dream

I have a dream,
A dream that gives second chances to everyone
I believe in world peace
I have a dream
To emancipate black people
To save some countries from poverty
To help those in need

If I had one wish
I would wish for world peace
If people didn't judge on looks the world would be a better place
I believe in respect for every human being
There's good in everyone
It doesn't matter if we're black or white, we're still human
Only God can judge us.

People lose hope easily
If we look inside ourselves and be strong
We'll finally see the truth

We should stand up to what we believe in
Stand up for love
Stand up for life

The world would be peace
If there was no jealousy
No hatred for each other

If we see a human suffering we should
Give them a drink of water and help them
We should not judge them
They may have done wrong
We should give them a second chance
Mother Teresa helped all those in need
Mother Teresa has inspired me

Love all like brothers and sisters

I have a dream
For everyone in the world to have food
Not be selfish

I have a dream
Martin Luther King had a dream
Tupac Shakur had a dream

Rest in peace Martin Luther King
Rest in peace Tupac Shakur.

Mousumi Choudhury (12)
High Ridge Specialist Sports College

I Have A Dream

I had a dream that I would win the lottery,
But now I have a dream that crime will be banished,
I don't know how but I will,
I don't know when but I will.

I had a dream that I would be king,
But now I have a dream that guns will just simply dissolve,
I don't know how but I will,
I don't know when but I will.

I know this will take a while,
Especially with no help,
But when I achieve these goals, I can sleep,
Knowing that the people of Earth are safe and sound.

Adam Catley (11)
High Ridge Specialist Sports College

I Have A Dream

I have a dream, it is very bright,
That every person black or white
Holds hands and reunite.

We are all humans
Known in some relations,
Sister, brother, mother, father,
Daughters and sons,
We all share the same emotions
Generation after generation.

I have a dream, the world in harmony, no fights, no rioting
And definitely no biting!

I have a dream so lovely and nice,
There is no difference between black or white.

We love all the colours of the rainbow
Individual and bright.

I have a dream that black and white coloured people are proud
And shot it out loud!

People helping each other and feeling good,
Having fun together in the mud!

I have a dream that is very positive,
People from different backgrounds with good motives
Working together no matter what disability,
Achieving better in simplicity.

Ayesha Begum (13)
High Ridge Specialist Sports College

I Have A Dream!

Motherless baby and babyless mother
Bring them together to love one another.

Dirty place, clean place,
Which do you prefer?
Clean of course, but some don't have that.
Starved or full?
Dry or thirsty?
Instead of people dying from these things.

I have a dream,
Let people die feeling good,
Why not get washed?
Then you'll have dignity,
When you are on your way,
Instead of people dying from these things.

I have a dream that
When you see
Homeless people
Ill or dirty,
Why not give them the treatment they need,
Instead of people dying from these things.

I have a dream,
If people aren't your colour,
It does not matter.
Still give them the help they need
Even if they're your enemy,
Instead of people dying from these things.

I have a dream,
People getting diseases,
Dying every second, every minute, every day,
To give them the treatment,
To give them homes.
Contact people as quick as you can,
Instead of people dying from these things.

If life could just be like this,
Then this is my dream!

Gemma Atterby (12)
High Ridge Specialist Sports College

My Great Dream

My dream is to have no wars
Where people obey us and laws,
No fighting, killing or any other,
Treat each other like sister or brother.

My dream is to have no poaching
Animals like Bengal tigers and pandas,
Being hunted down to extinction,
There's a low chance of distinction.

My dream is to have no terrorism or any other,
That is my dream . . . not any other.

Nicholas Hutchinson (12)
High Ridge Specialist Sports College

I Have A Dream

I have a dream,
No poverty, no war, no diseases.
I have a dream,
No racism, no shooting, nor battle.
Third World countries dying because of starvation,
Dying because of disease,
Dying because of poverty.

Look at their faces,
Their eyes,
See the hunger,
See the war,
See life through their eyes.

Rebekah Hirst (12)
High Ridge Specialist Sports College

I Have A Dream!

I have a dream
That all people get treatment,
There is no need for people to suffer,
The WHO have the money.

I have a dream,
Even if you're poor
You don't have to wait,
Not for treatment anyway.

I have a dream
People live healthily,
Maybe more medication,
I don't like seeing people dying.

I have a dream
That even Third World countries live happily,
Not just the rich,
It's not fair!

Jemma Reid (12)
High Ridge Specialist Sports College

I Have A Dream

I have a dream that the world
Could be embellished in peace.

I have a dream that the bullies could stop
Being belligerent and give others respect.

I have a dream that everybody could be treated
The same and not judged by looks.

I have a dream that there was no poverty
And people on the street were sheltered by caring people.

I have a dream today.

Jason Stephenson (12)
High Ridge Specialist Sports College

I Have A Dream!

I have a dream
That all people will have a family,
Will have a bed to rest
And love to share.

I have a dream
That no one will suffer from starvation,
Everyone will live healthily
And help each other.

I have a dream
That there won't be a difference
Between rich and poor,
Or black and white
Because everyone will love one another.

I have a dream
That the world will be like a beautiful garden,
No more wars to spoil it
So that the plants and animals
Can live happily just like us.

I have a dream
That the world
Will be more than perfect.

This is my dream.

Cátia Vaz (13)
High Ridge Specialist Sports College

Let's Dream

More money to the world,
The Third World countries,
They need money
And it's not funny.

I have a dream . . .
I have a dream . . .
Just one dream . . .

Let's send food and water
Plus medicine,
Let's also stop the war,
The kids are really sore.

I have a dream . . .
I have a dream . . .
Just one dream . . .

Can you *hear* them scream?

Louis Finch (13)
High Ridge Specialist Sports College

Peace

I dream that the world was embellished
With freedom from pain,
With free-flowing, non polluted seas.
Rest in peace my beloved souls,
Fly to the clouds above,
Like a graceful turtle dove.

The first world is banal.
The Third World is wise.
I dream that everyone has love and freedom.
I wish the word belligerent would be erased
And the world would come together
To form a loving human race.

I had a dream today.

Jordan Grace (12)
High Ridge Specialist Sports College

My Dream

I want to give the world peace,
Let it be a better place
For us to live in.

I want the world to have no war,
No mess, no killing
And be a tidy and happy place
For us to live in.

I want the world to be beautiful,
No rubbish, just wonderful.

I want all the people in the world to have no
Bad people, just nice loving people.

This is how I want the world to be,
Wonderful and peaceful.

Hayley Houldridge (13)
High Ridge Specialist Sports College

I Have A Dream

I have a dream . . .
I have the power to change the world,
Now the sails of power have unfurled,
I have the power, I have the muscles,
As your leader I will never need Brussels,
As your leader there will be no war,
As your leader violence will be used no more,
As your leader there is no need to live in fear,
For as your leader, I will be here,
If only, if only,
I could believe my dream.
I could use it for good or use it for bad,
I could make people feel happy or make them feel sad.
If only, if only,
My dream was real . . .

Adam Cunningham (12)
King's School

No Spk Eng

I hv a drm, whr ppl cn spk proprly,
Nstd ov usng jrgn,
& tlkng ttl rbbsh.
Its vry frstrtng, &
I h8 it al.
Wots evry1s prblm?
Th Eng lang hz evlvd ovr thsnds ov yrs,
Frm lng ded, & out ov use dilcts,
Combnng nfluncs frm so mny othr srces,
Bt luk @ us al now
Wot hv we bcom?
I wz on a trn th othr dy, whn I saw a gy txtng sum1.
He wz usng txt lang & I jst wntd 2 stnd up & say,
'Oi! Stp it, 4 gds sak!'
I ddnt.
Bt mayb I shud hav, it wud hv mde him thnk 4 a chng.
Hw mch tim dos evry1 need 2 sav in spch,
Only 2 los it al agn in th tim it taks 2 intrprt?
My dream is rather erudite.

Richard Baker (17)
King's School

I Have A Dream

Zoom, zoom up to 1st,
Hope my nitros will not burst.
Hope the police do not see me,
Or I will have to flee,
Jumping over boats,
Trying not to land and float.

Charles Lawson (12)
Middlefield School

I Have A Dream

I have a dream
Without war,
No killing or cheating at all.

I have a dream
All were friends
Helping each other all the time.

I have a dream
With no world hunger,
Where people shared all,
No one alone.

No pollution,
Fresh air.

Maiken Lynggaard (13)
Middlefield School

I Have A Dream

I have a dream
That one day I will
Fly high and low
And go with the flow.

Fly high in the clouds
And still be as loud,
So people will notice me
And when I get back they offer me a cup of tea.

When out there
I will strike like a cobra,
And flee the scene as quick as a cheetah,
So that's what I want to do.

Join the RAF.

Robert Craven (13)
Middlefield School

I Have A Dream

I have a dream
That I would be seen,
For all my talents.
The world would be balanced,
No more wars,
This is what I will adore.
No more hunting,
Then I would be chanting,
Oh joy, oh joy, oh joy.

Ryan Morton (12)
Middlefield School

I Have A Dream

Last night I had this dream:
The wind was whistling in the air,
The darkness cold and sharp
And in the dusty, foggy night,
A cold and dim figure was walking towards me.

I couldn't move, I couldn't scream,
I couldn't take my eyes off it,
Fear rustling hairs on the back of my neck
And then more figures and more and more
And I screamed until I felt the cold wind suffocate me.

But then a gunshot and one fell,
In slow motion I saw a bullet clip my ear
And when I turned to see who had rescued me
Nothing but darkness and I knew I was alone once more,
It swallowed me like a giant mouth.

And then I woke up, sweating but cold,
I turn on my light to get my eyes adjusted to my room,
But it wasn't my room, it was nothing like it
And I was lost in this nightmare,
This nightmare that could kill me if I let fear in.

So I counted to 5 aloud very slowly,
I let fear in for 5 seconds.
'1, 2, 3, 4, 5.' I opened my ears,
My room, my house, my family, my teddy bears
But something was wrong and the suspicion was piercing my brain.

Helen Burton (13)
Middlefield School

I Have A Dream

Looking at the planes flying so high,
Up above in the big blue sky,
Taking off from the ground,
Making lots and lots of sound,
Speeding up to fly around,
Trying to break the speed of sound,
Taking down some fighter planes,
Some of them go insane,
Crashing down in the sea,
I wonder what they think of me.

Daryl Jefferson (12)
Middlefield School

I Have A Dream

I have a dream
And in that dream
There was a world
And in that world
There was a house
And in that house
There was a girl.

I had a dream last night,
It was really bright,
It was about the woman I admire
Achieving her desire.
I was in that dream,
There was a really big scream,
The woman shouted
And then she pouted,
They had told her what she could be,
They said she could be on TV.
This is how she became a model,
She got in really easy.
My dream finished
And that was the end.

Lauren Shepherd (12)
Middlefield School

I Have A Dream

I have a dream that the world would be peaceful,
No bad and tough like a bull.
The skies would be clear,
Everyone would have no fear.
The sun would glisten
And people who have problems tell others and they will listen.
For our lives to be better
And our worries to go away,
But this is only a dream
And life is a reality so this won't come true!

Jessica Hodson (13)
Middlefield School

I Had A Dream

I had a dream
Everything was made out of chocolate.
I had a dream
That most things were pink and sparkly.
I had a dream
No one ever fights and there's no wars.
I had a dream
Everyone was loaded with money.
I had a dream
There was no school.
I had a dream
That I go shopping every day.
I had a dream
It was summer every day.
I had a dream
The sky was all pink!

Katie Gleadell (12)
Middlefield School

I Have A Dream

Angel, angel I have a dream,
Angel, angel it is so supreme,
'Tis not like any other,
In this dream I have a brother,
I have a family,
I have a family,
It's like the size of Doncaster Dome.

I have a name,
This dream is like a game,
I have a job,
This dream is sent by God,
It is a message,
'Tis from the Lord,
I am a boy
Yet I feel so bored.

I feel so loved
Right down to the core,
I have a house that has a door,
I feel so safe,
I look in the mirror,
I see a face,
I see not a boy but a man,
This could be a dream,
I have a plan,
I will sleep
Never to wake,
When the world ends
I will just lie and bake,
I would rather die in my dream,
Oh yes, this dream is so supreme.

Alex Malone (13)
Middlefield School

I Have A Dream

My dream is a Pagani Zonda,
Speeding down in the yonder,
Hearing the 6.0 litre V8 screech,
And it sucks the petrol like a leech,
Looking at the shiny chrome wheels,
So cool it attracts the seals,
0 to 60 in 2.5 seconds
And it's a better car than David Beckham's,
I always go for an ice cream in my monster machine,
That's my dream.
Oh, one more thing, it's always clean.

Joshua Stringwell
Middlefield School

I Have A Dream!

I have a dream
to be a policeman.
I have a dream
to be a judge.
I have a dream
to drive a car.
I have a dream
to be a paramedic.
I have a dream
to be a truck driver.
I have a dream
to be a crash investigator.
I have a dream
to be a person who fixes computers.
I have a dream
to live my life in peace.
I have a dream
to be a train driver.
I have a dream
I want to be an FBI agent.
I have a dream
to be a secret agent.
I have a dream
to drive a tank for the first time.
I have a dream
to fire a gun.
I have a dream
to be a rally driver.
I have a dream
This is how I want to live my life.

Kieron Cole (13)
Middlefield School

I Have A Dream

As I yawn, ready for bed,
Thoughts and dreams enter my head,
Away from reality and into a dream,
Mountains of chocolate and crystal streams,
My world of wonder, has come true,,
My imagination, has now flew,
Off its wings and into the sky,
It feels so real as I fly,
The wind flowing through my hair,
I have no worries or a care,
There are no cages, I am free,
To be what I want to be,
My dream is a special place,
Everyone is happy, not a sad face,
In my dreams I can cheat death,
I always have one lost breath,
My dreams escape all fears and lies,
The morning sun, reflects in my eyes,
All my friends here beside me,
It's better than reality,
My dreams are an amazing sight,
From sunrise, to the deep dark night,
I'm so happy, I'm floating on a feather,
Wishing my dreams could last forever,
My beautiful world, I have created,
Everything to me is gold plated,
My special place is here for me,
And will be for eternity,
Suddenly my alarm goes off, my dream drifts away,
I'll be back . . . another day.

Chelsea Terry (14)
Middlefield School

I Have A Dream

I have a dream,
A dream to play for Chelsea,
A dream to meet Frank Lampard,
I have a dream.

I have a dream,
A dream to drive the fastest car,
A dream to beat all my friends,
That's what you call a dream.

I have a dream,
A dream to be a go-kart racer,
A dream to change the mini-tyres,
I have a dream.

I have a dream,
A dream that I own a mansion,
A dream to have any cars in the big garage,
That's what you call a dream.

Then I woke up!

Steven Spindley (11)
Middlefield School

Keep It

Hope, dreams from when you were born,
All gone, nothing.
Wealth, riches everything to have,
All gone, nothing.
Ownership, lordship, everything to rule,
All gone, nothing.
Money, companies, everything to own,
All gone, nothing.
Fun, great times, freedom,
All here, keep it.
Love, happiness, joy,
All here, keep it.
Laughter, memories and friends,
All of the good things,
Keep it.

Edward Wood (11)
Queen Elizabeth's Grammar School

I Wish

Peace, what of it is there in the world?
I wish I could change it.
Life for someone in a country filled with war
Is like a feather,
Thin, weightless,
It grows and is cast off,
A heartbroken bird lies dead whereas the feather is blown away
                                                        to be killed.

Poverty,
I wish I could change it
Like a comb running through unwashed hair,
It runs through everything nasty and dry,
Nothing luscious or delicious to pick up,
Just dry horrible wasteland.

Cruelty, towards any living being,
I wish I could change it,
It is like a pebble,
It is cast out into the sea,
No one caring about it,
It is made redundant by its own true form.

I wish I had 3 wishes.

William Kinnon (11)
Queen Elizabeth's Grammar School

Constantly Thinking

Constantly thinking,
Thinking of another world,
A better place.

Constantly seeing,
Seeing the look on a
Homeless child's face.

Constantly dreaming,
Dreaming of a world
Without war.

Constantly imagining,
Imagining a world without hunger,
Where no one was poor.

The glass eyes stare,
As they wish,
As they hope,
With doubt,
Living without.

Louise Spence (12)
Queen Elizabeth's Grammar School

My Magical Place

I have a dream of a magical place,
Nothing bad there takes place.
Everyone's free and no one's at war,
No rich, no poor.
People have friends and no one's alone,
Beautiful weather keeps everything in tone.
All the flowers and all the trees,
Make it a wonderful place for the honeybees.
Rivers and streams flow quietly by,
While all sorts of birds fly through the sky.
The sun's rays warm my back,
As I walk along a winding track.
With the breeze rustling through the leaves,
The babbling brook wanders and weaves.

Alyssia Rawlins (12)
Queen Elizabeth's Grammar School

If I Could . . .

If I could do just one thing to help the world,
I would help people in Africa with problems like drought,
Long hot days drag by, burning anything in their sight,
Hard, dry cracked land with hardly any waterholes,
Hunger and drought sweep over all of Africa,
Like a black hole stealing people's lives,
People die leaving loved ones alone,
Fun and joy long gone,
The future looks bleak,
Time's running out.

Sarah Carroll (12)
Queen Elizabeth's Grammar School

Break The Silence

I wonder if the world was free
I would change a lot if it were up to me.
I'd give the silence a voice of gold
Instead of an iron tight mould.
I would rip apart the cruel, cruel space
Between the rich and poor,
But what about those still in the silence.
A mind given to them by someone else,
A puppet of hate and loathing, shouted at,
Pushed down, nothing at all, nothing of significance.
But they all have a voice inside,
Let them break away from their cages of shadows.

Eleanor Redwood (12)
Queen Elizabeth's Grammar School

Blurred Vision

She stood there.
Just staring.
Not wanting to believe.
Her hands,
Her face,
Her clothes,
Encrusted in brown dirt.
One second,
That was all it had taken.
Everything she knew,
Everything she loved,
Gone,
In one second.
She tried to pick out,
A single memory,
Of what it was like,
Before the bombs,
Before the guns,
Before the dying,
Before the thing,
That should never have happened,
Before what she couldn't stop.
But only,
Blurred vision.

Charlotte Slade (12)
Queen Elizabeth's Grammar School

Happiness

Happiness is everything . . .
Being with friends and family,
People going to work and school,
Rushing around,
Having sweets and chocolates, *yum-yum!*
At the weekend . . .
Playing in the garden, lovely and warm,
Seeing your favourite footy team play,
Birthdays, weddings, Christmas and Easter too,
Listening to music and dancing around!
The world is full of happiness,
Hope you are too!

Emily Walker (11)
Queen Elizabeth's Grammar School

No Access

This girl could never change the whole world,
But she could always bring a bright spark to mine.
Though she may be younger and smaller than me,
I look up to her in every way.
I feel as if I don't see her very often,
And that I have no access,
But really I know that I can talk to her whenever I like.
She will always be with me through good and bad times,
And I respect her for that more than anything else.
So, she may not be able to change everyone's lives,
But she has certainly changed mine in so many ways.

She's the girl I can always rely on,
The person who puts a smile on my face,
The one I will love forever,
Keri.

Amy Clark (12)
Queen Elizabeth's Grammar School

Independence Day

I saw the look of
Anxiety in his face
In the seconds
Before
The start of the race
That urge to win
To at least be
In the top three
For his friends
And family
He heard the gun go
He heard the crowd scream
And ran like a dream
He was floating
Released
Freely treading
The charged air
No pressure
No one to judge
Their watchful eyes
Dragging him down
Every loss a frown
Upon a perfect surface
To take the one chance
And seize it
To choose to be free
And independent.

Touchdown.

Rebekah Smith (12)
Queen Elizabeth's Grammar School

My Dreams

My dreams go through the roof,
Into the sky,
Into space,
Hoping that they will never die.

My dreams are happy,
My dreams are sad,
To see poor people in the world
Just drives me mad.

My dreams are peaceful,
Sometimes deep,
Wars rage on,
Without relief.

My dreams are in my head
While I lay,
People die from starvation
Every day.

My dreams are so small,
The disasters so grand,
What can be done,
To save this land?

If everyone joined together
We could make a difference,
Surely, that would change the world?

Alex Temple-Marsh (12)
Queen Elizabeth's Grammar School

Changes

War is thrown away like a pebble,
Poverty is disabled,
Malice is cut by the cable,
Hate is tipped off the table,
Crime collapses as it is too unstable,
Evil is not enabled,
Swearing is taken out with a ladle,
Prejudice is crystallised like treacle,
Racism is thrown out the cradle,
Fear is just a fable,
Sadness is unstapled.

Ross Pallister (11)
Queen Elizabeth's Grammar School

He Said

'I'm going to erase poverty,' he said,
Using his head.
'I'm going to erase world hunger,' he said
Giving everyone some bread.
'I'm going to erase the war,' he said,
As he bled.
'I'm going to erase taxes,' he said,
Not being fed,
About to be dead,
His face went red,
As he bled,
In his bed.
'He'll be dead,' they said,
'They'll 'ave his head,' the said.
'There will be peace,'
He told his niece.
'War will decrease,' he said,
Once again, using his head.
Those were the last words of the man who led,
As he bled,
In his bed.
'He'll be dead,' they said,
'They'll 'ave his head,' they said.

Andy Reid (11)
Queen Elizabeth's Grammar School

.

Insignificant

I saw
The red-hot malice.
Watched it trickle down his
Pale, pinched chin.
A single droplet,
A droplet that told me everything.
I knew the words
Bubbling ferociously behind those lips.
Cold,
Hard,
Merciless,
But then I think.
Everything,
If this was everything
Then what is nothing?
Nothing is the person
Who never shows their face?
The innocent child
With the bruise on their knee?
And the rest?
So maybe nothing is everything
And the meaning of everything
Is nothing.
And nothing lies
In a black abyss
Of no one.
Nothing, break free,
Free from all,
Forever.

And then he said it.

Megan Dalton (11)
Queen Elizabeth's Grammar School

I Had A Dream, That . . .

I had a dream,
    That going out in the dark,
        Was only scary because of imaginary monsters.

I had a dream,
    That mothers wouldn't fear,
        When letting their beloved children play out on the
                        park swings.

I had a dream,
    That talking to a stranger,
        Is not a dangerous thing to do, it's making a new friend.

I had a dream,
    That the title of bad-guy,
        Was only used in films, and the superheroes were real.

I had a dream,
    That the sound of the gunshot,
        Was just a car backfiring and not the cold silence
                        of death.

I had a dream,
    That what we see on the news,
        Is of love, courage and peace, not hate, fear
                        and suffering.

I had a dream,
    That when I lie down at night,
        I'm safe in my covers, my bubble of fantasy, my dream.

I had a dream,
    That should be reality,
        And it would be, if *love* were allowed to rule
                        human nature.

Isabel Windeatt (15)
The Humberston School

Believe

One day in your lifetime,
Someone will say,
You have to climb a mountain,
If you don't you'll regret it.

If you try when you can do,
There is no need to cry,
Do what you have to,
To achieve what you want to.

There is no need to panic,
No need to act manic,
You can hang with some crew,
But don't let them tell you what to do.

If you believe in others,
You can go very far,
If you believe in yourself,
You can reach the stars.

Rosie Birkinshaw (12)
The Humberston School

A Dreamer

I am a dreamer,
A dreamer you will find,
I dream all day, I dream all night,
Some amazing dreams I've found.

So once I had a wonderful dream
Of what I want to be.

I dreamt I taught some children
In drama or PE,
I hope I do, oh I hope I do become
A success story.

A small sweet child from primary
To secondary, then turned to a teacher,
A success just waiting to be!

Megan Garner (11)
Vale of Ancholme Technology College

I Have A Dream

I have a dream . . .
I have a dream racism will cease,
I have a dream to begin world peace.

I have a dream . . .
I have a dream children can wake up in warm beds in a safe place
And all people will have the potential to follow their dreams.

I have a dream to end all bullying,
I have a dream to help all people,
I have a dream to protect innocent people from the forces of evil,
I have a dream . . .

Hannah Wilson (12)
Vale of Ancholme Technology College

The Dream

This world: blemished and bruised
With the suffering of these children, cursed with famine.

The war: like two cats fighting over a scrap of skate
Raging rapidly, adding to this curse.

The dream: to stop this curse, scarping the darkness away from

this world,
To reveal the light and help these souls.

We could do this, friend. You and I could make a difference.

We can, you and I,
We could turn this world around,
We can, you and I.

Liam Arnold (13)
Western Technology School

I Have A Dream!

I have a dream,
Dream's an image,
I think about them and laugh in my head, it comes true.

Bad dreams about horrible things,
Scary, bad, bloody and black.

Good dreams about
My friends and family,
Going out and having fun.

Kelly Wright (13)
Western Technology School

I Have A Dream

Under the hot and beautiful sun
There is a group of Africans
With flies on their faces
And no shoes.
I have a dream of all people
Being treated equal
With homes to live in.

Under the plant of pins is golden sand
But no water, not a drop around.
I have a dream that
There's fresh water everywhere
Even in a sink.

Under the sand are plants,
Next to the plants are ants,
With mouths to chop on your feet
I have a dream of shoes on every foot
So the ants won't make you dance.

In the dead of the night there is a
Fight that sounds like a
Train going fast and turns into pain.
I have a dream where
Violence is banned,
Everyone is at peace,
These are the dreams that I dreamed.

If you make my dream reality
I will die a happy man.

Thomas Cole (12)
Western Technology School

The Blast Of A Bomb

I have a dream
Everything has gone
Blast of a bomb
People lost lives
From terrible lies
Horrible heights
Dark nights

Kids lay alone
With no home
Parents gone
Blast of a bomb
No food or drink
So just have a think

Remember what you've got
And they have not
Electricity, fashion
They've got passion
All that's left is a memory
That's temporary

Just give them a thought.

Lauren O'Neill (13)
Western Technology School

Rations Of Dreams!

W ars, street fights, gunners and more,
O rdinary people sent to war,
R unning and fighting for their lives,
L ittle teenage criminals holding knives,
D rugs and murders none of this needed!

P eace and love is what we need,
E veryone isn't born to plead,
A re we all getting irate?
C ataclysm, death and fate,
E verything needs to stop.

I dentifying the bodies,
S o souls are set free.

G reat dreams are still there,
R oasting, flying everywhere,
E arth doesn't need this mess,
A nd can I stop this? *Yes!*
T ime flies when you have good dreams!

Bronwen Roberts (13)
Western Technology School

Poem . . . My Dreams

My dreams are exciting,
Full of inspiration and power,
Bright and beaming,
I can hardly see.

Waiting for my dreams to come true,
I relax and remember what my life is really like.
Daydreams, life changing dreams,
Or just dreams
If only one came true.

My dreams are long,
I dream all the time,
My life gets better;
Brighter than sunshine.

Victoria Betmead (13)
Western Technology School

Dreams

I have a dream
That all the war will stop,
No more poverty and all hunger will stop.

I have a dream,
That all the poor will get money
And rich would not be greedy.

I have a dream,
That all the thieves and pickpockets get gone,
Have to pay and give all things back.

'I have a dream!'

Shannon Turner (12)
Western Technology School

I Have A Dream!

I have a dream where
Everything is in darkness and everybody's sleeping,
We suddenly hear this horrific beeping,
As we jump to our feet we hear it!
Guns shooting, bombs booming,
Everybody crying for help!

It's started again, the war has begun,
We hear the planes come back,
The bombs are banging and blowing things up,
I sit crying and want it to be over.

After a few months, it all goes quiet,
Is this it I hope, it's over,
I step out of my shelter, it's horrible!
The houses are wrecked and the paths are gone,
I fear for all the children.

I have a dream where
People are injured, guns everywhere,
Bombs all over the floor.
We can all rest now and live in peace,
Until they come back for more.

I wake in hot sweats, it was just a dream,
The people all helped to protect our land,
They can't come back I tell myself,
So I close my eyes and fall back into a deep sleep.

Jodie Blakey (13)
Western Technology School

War And Peace

War is one big bomb
Banging and booming,
It's scary.
War, people dying,
Getting hurt and burned,
What's it worth?

Peace on a quiet day,
No noise, no movement,
It's perfect.
Peace, the time of quiet,
No war, no guns,
Just a dream?

Amber Bell (13)
Western Technology School

Dreams

Dreams are a thing that
You want to happen.
Dreams are a thing
You have to imagine,
They are things you desire.

A dream is a thing you want to do,
A dream is a thing you want to see,
A dream is a desire.

My dream is that
No one is alone in the world.
My dream is that
Life is longer to do more.
My dream is that
Life is worth living.

What is your dream?

Kirstie-Rose Gilbert (12)
Western Technology School